The D-Day War Diaries

JUNO BEACH

CANADIAN 3RD ARMY DIVISION DEPLOYMENTS

THE ALLIED OPERATION TO RECOVER EUROPE FROM GERMAN OCCUPATION

James Robertshaw

CONTENTS

Prologue v

Forward vii

Chapter 1
Operation Overlord 1

Chapter 2
Canadian 3rd Army Division 4
Training and Formation

Chapter 3
Canadian 3rd Division 6
Preparations & Plan

Chapter 4
Canadian 3rd Division Units 9
Casualties and Commanders

Chapter 5
Canadian 3rd Division 15
Actions and Operations

Chapter 6
German Forces and Units 16
Defensive Positions

Chapter 7
    German Forces Units 22
    Commanders

Chapter 8
    French Resistance Operations 23
    & Special Operations Executive

Chapter 9
    RCAF Bombing Operations 25

Chapter 10
    Royal Canadian Naval Operations 26

Chapter 11
    D-Day Actions 28
    Write up on Landings

Chapter 12
    D-Day Actions 31

Chapter 13
    List of Citations. 38

Chapter 14
    Current Museums & Plaques 39

Copyright © 2023 James Robertshaw

All rights reserved. This book or any portion thereof may not be reproduced or used in any manner whatsoever without the express written permission of the publisher except for the use of brief quotations in a book review.

Printed by LULU Books

First printing 2023

ISBN 978-1-9161841-8-3

James Robertshaw

Publisher

www.dday-wardiaries.co.uk

PROLOGUE

I was inspired to write this booklet after visiting the D-Day beaches with my twin brother John in March 2014, the 70th Anniversary of the D-Day landings.

I hope you find it interesting and inspiring to visit and buy the other booklets. I was moved with the sites and graves of all my past fellow countrymen and what they did for the freedom of mankind and my country.

I have decided to donate the profits to the Royal British Legion and Combat Stress.

This is the second booklet trying to give factual information of what happened on that first day.

James Robertshaw

This book, as one in the series, is specifically created to not only inform those younger members of society of the great sacrifices our service personnel made in World War II, but also to add support to our service personnel of today.

FORWARD

"You will bring about the destruction of the German war machine, the elimination of Nazi tyranny over the oppressed peoples of Europe and security for ourselves in a free world. Your task will not be an easy one. Your enemy is well trained, well equipped and battle-hardened. He will fight savagely. The free men of the world are marching together to victory. I have full confidence in your courage, devotion to duty and skill in battle. We will accept nothing less than full victory. Good luck, and let us all beseech the blessings of Almighty God upon this great and noble undertaking."

General Dwight D. Eisenhower giving the D-Day order on June 6, 1944.

PAINTING A PICTURE OF THE OPERATION

The landings had been postponed for several days due to bad weather. When the order was given to "Go", the weather was still bad.

The men boarded the ships and set off. A lot of men were sea sick, but spirits were high, the weapons were checked and the first units landed to deal with their objectives. The casualties in the first units 8th and 9th Infantry Brigades were lighter than other D-Day Operations because of the 40 DD Sherman tanks of the 6th and 10th Armoured Brigades that landed with them and cut down casualties. We have documented the actions and citations so one can appreciate the efforts and sacrifices that were made by our troops.

God Bless them.

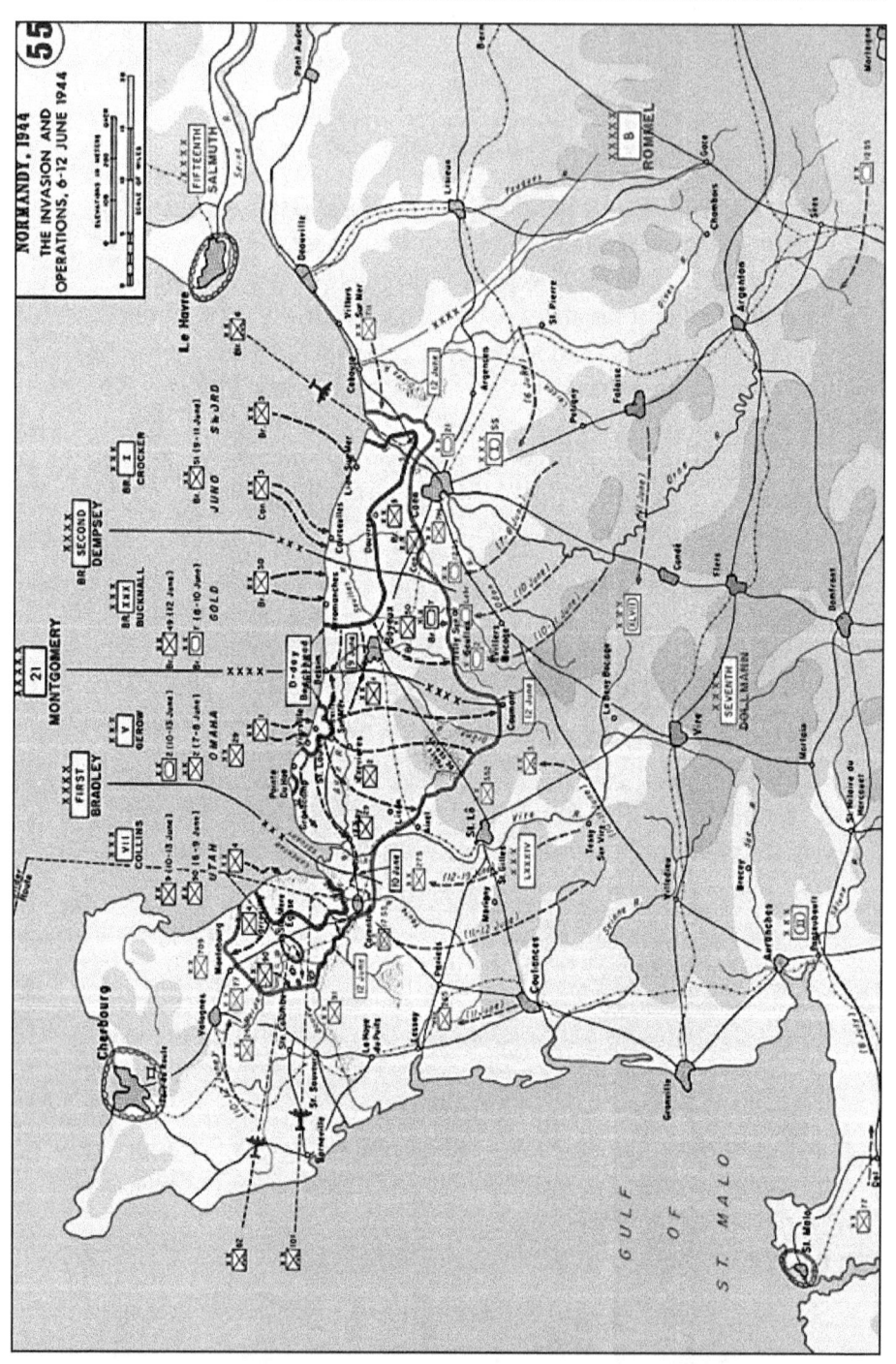

CHAPTER 1

OPERATION OVERLORD

The allied operation to recover Europe from German Occupation, decided at Casablanca Conference in 1943, between Churchill, Roosevelt and Stalin. The landings were forced by Stalin at the Tehran Conference in December 1943 to relieve the pressure on Russia from the Axis troops.

It took three years to plan the invasion and gather materials and was a multi national effort on behalf of the Allies, gathering men, materials, aircraft and ships together to mount an invasion and start the Western front.

Three million men in total — In the first wave of D-Day, three hundred thousand men with seven thousand ships.

The Canadian 3rd Division's task was to secure the Juno landing beaches and then cut the Caen-Bayeux and seize Carpiquet Airport west of Caen. The main landing beaches where Sword – (British), Juno – (Canadian), Gold – (British), Omaha (U.S.), Utah – (U.S.) and the western flank was protected by the US 101st and 82nd Airborne. These are the subject of separate publications.

The invasion was postponed due to bad weather and eventually General Eisenhower, Supreme Allied Commander gave the order "Go" for the early hours of June 6th 1944 for the invasions to start. Midget submarines (X-23) were launched to guide ships to the beaches and the RAF started their bombing runs. The BBC put out coded messages to the French Resistance to activate units to disrupt German communication and transport. Fields of barbed wire and mines covered the beaches with lots of beach obstacles, no easy task.

Left: Map showing D-Day Beaches.
3rd Canadian Infantry Division was under 1st Corps Lieutenant General Crocker, part of the 2nd British Army under Lieutenant General Dempsey.

CANADIAN BEACHES & GOALS.

The task of the Canadian 3rd Army was to capture the landing beaches and make their way inland to cut the Bayeux-Caen road and take the Carpiquet Airport west of Caen. German fortifications had to be taken first.

There were three objectives that had to be achieved by the Canadian 3rd Division for D-Day, under the overall command of Major General Roderick Keller. Objective lines as follows on Map.

1st Objective – Code name 'Yew' – St Aubin-sur-Mer to Reviers.

2nd Objective – Code name 'Elm' – Creully to Colomby-sur-Thaon.

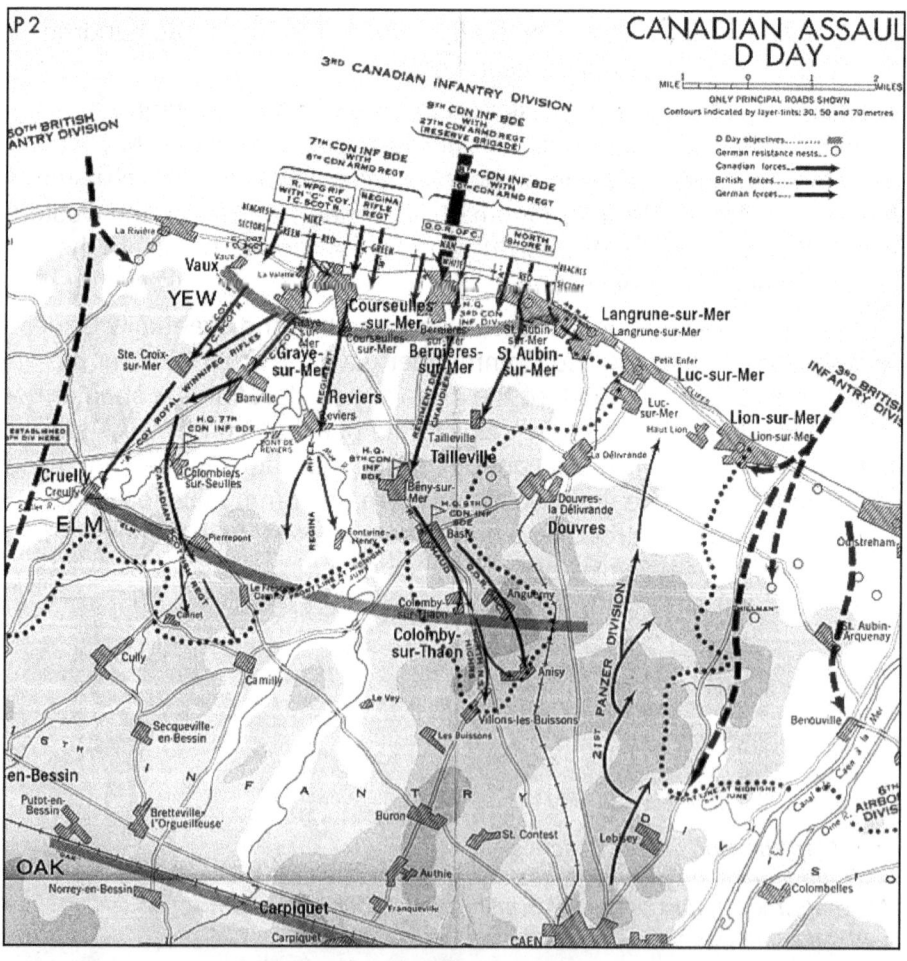

JUNO BEACH — CANADIAN 3ʳᴰ ARMY DIVISION

3ʳᵈ Objective – Code name 'Oak' – Putot-en-Bessin to Carpiquet Aéroport.

Three attacking brigades – task forces – №48 Royal Marines link with Sword

1. 7ᵗʰ Brigade + 1ˢᵗ Hussars (6ᵗʰ Armoured) 40 DD Tanks – West Sector.
2. 8ᵗʰ Brigade + Fort Garry (10ᵗʰ Armoured) 40 DD Tanks – East Sector.
3. 9ᵗʰ Brigade + Sherbrooke Fusiliers (27ᵗʰ Armoured) 40 DD Tanks – Carpiquet Airport.

The landing beaches stretched from Lion-sur-Mer (edge of Sword Beach) to Asnelles (edge of Gold Beach). Juno Beach was split into various sectors as follows: –

Nan East Flank – landed Nan Red – marched to Lagrune-sur-Mer №48 Royal Marine Commando.

Nan Red – St Aubin-sur-Mer, 8ᵗʰ Canadian Infantry Brigade with 10ᵗʰ Armoured Brigade – North Shore (New Brunswick Regiment). A and B Companies, Le Régiment de la Chaudière. Fort Gary Tank (10ᵗʰ Armoured).

Nan White – Bernieres, 8ᵗʰ Canadian Infantry Brigade with 10ᵗʰ Armoured Brigade – Queens Own Rifles of Canada, (A and B Companies), Fort Garry Tanks, Le Régiment de la Chaudière.

Nan Green – Corseulles-sur-Mer – 7ᵗʰ Infantry Brigade with 6ᵗʰ Armoured – Regina Rifles (A and B Company), with 1ˢᵗ Hussars (6ᵗʰ Armoured).

Mike Red – Graye-sur-Mer – 7ᵗʰ Infantry Brigade with 6ᵗʰ Armoured – Royal Winnipeg Rifles A and B Companies, 1ˢᵗ Battalion Canadian Scottish (Pierrepoint) (A Company), with 1ˢᵗ Hussars (6ᵗʰ Armoured).

Mike Green – La Valette and Vaux – 7ᵗʰ Infantry Brigade with 6ᵗʰ Armoured, Royal Winnipeg Rifles (C and D Companies), 1ˢᵗ Battalion Canadian Scottish (C Company) with 1ˢᵗ Hussars.

In Reserve 2ⁿᵈ Wave 9ᵗʰ Infantry Brigade with 27ᵗʰ Armoured Regiment the Sherbrooke Fusiliers.

CHAPTER 2

CANADIAN 3RD ARMY DIVISION TRAINING AND FORMATION

Maj General Keller

The Canadian Division located in bases in Hampshire, England in 1943-44. The formation was supported by the 2nd Canadian Armoured Brigade and additional units, under **Major General Roderick Keller.**

18th of August 1942 – **Operation Jubilee** the raid on Dieppe, was a rehearsal for the D-Day Landings. It was also a secret mission by the SAS and Royal Marines to capture the new German Codebook from the German Dieppe HQ for Bletchley Park under Royal Navy Commander Ian Fleming.

The 2nd Canadian Division under General Roberts learnt what went wrong following the casualty rate, out of 4,963 Canadian troops there were 3,369 casualties, (900 KIA and 1,944 taken prisoner). Revised training began in July 1943 under Harry Crerar commander of second Canadian Corp. Demanding training field exercises in Scotland in August and September 1943. Then with landing craft LCAs and LCTs and with DD Tanks through the winter.

CAMP	LOCATION	CAMP	LOCATION	CAMP	LOCATION
A1	Rowlands Castle	A12	Southwick	A18	Sarisbury
A2	Emsworth	A13	Farnham	A19	Gosport
A3	Portsmouth	A14	Westwalk	A20	Botley Common
A4	Horndene	A15	Wickham	C7	Hiltingbury
A10	Hambledon	A16	Funtley	C8	Chandlers Ford
A11	Denmead	A17	Bucklands		

War casualties on the beach at Dieppe

Raid on Dieppe, abandoned Scout Car

The King visits Canadian Scottish during training.

Briefing on the German Fortifications.

Tank training with Infantry.

CHAPTER 3

CANADIAN 3RD DIVISION PREPARATIONS & PLAN

The Germans had spent considerable time building up the Atlantic Wall to defend France against the Allies invasion of mainland Europe and the Western Front. At the Casablanca conference Churchill, Roosevelt and Stalin, agreed that they needed to land in Western Europe and plans were prepared from that day. Five beaches were targeted in Normandy, protected by Airborne troops to the East, 6th British Airborne and to the West the US 101st and 82nd Airborne. In order to fool the Germans and tie down troops the Allies launched a feint army under Major General Patton, the 1st US Army, to attack the Pas De Calais. Double agent Gabo working for the allies confirmed the deception to the Germans who were now convinced Normandy was a ruse and kept Panzer Divisions in the Pas De Calais. This tied down German Panzer Divisions. The strategy and plans the Allies followed for the invasion of Normandy were as follows.

RECONNAISSANCE OF THE AREA & THE BEACHES.

1. Quality of the beaches for landing.
2. Intelligence of German defences.
3. Combating German defences.
4. Disrupting reinforcements.
5. Training and formation of troops.

1. Beach obstacles used by the Germans – Mines, Hedgehogs, Stakes, Tank Ditches and Machine Gun Nests. This called for special equipment and also Royal Engineers to clear these obstacles.

2. Quality of the beaches for landing – The British used small midget submarines to check the quality of the beaches and also information from the local French Resistance. Major General Hobart was given the task of finding a solution. The 79th Armoured Division was formed to provide the equipment.

3   Intelligence of German Defences - this was gathered from the French Resistance, monitoring German radio signals, via Bletchley Park (code breakers) and the reconnaissance of the beaches and plotting of the German defences on army maps.

4   French Resistance – special coded messages were sent out on the BBC from London the day before D Day so that the French Resistance could disrupt communications and supply lines before the invasion. The Special Operations Executive sent out agents to co-ordinate these attacks. Many were rounded up and shot by the Germans.

5   Loading Ships from England - various ports were used and the fleet was protected by Allied Ships, bombers and minesweepers, departing on the night of the 5th of June 1944. German mines at sea also had to be cleared.

6   Briefing before landing.

CHAPTER 4
CANADIAN 3RD DIVISION UNITS
CASUALTIES AND COMMANDERS
OPERATION NEPTUNE   D-DAY LANDINGS

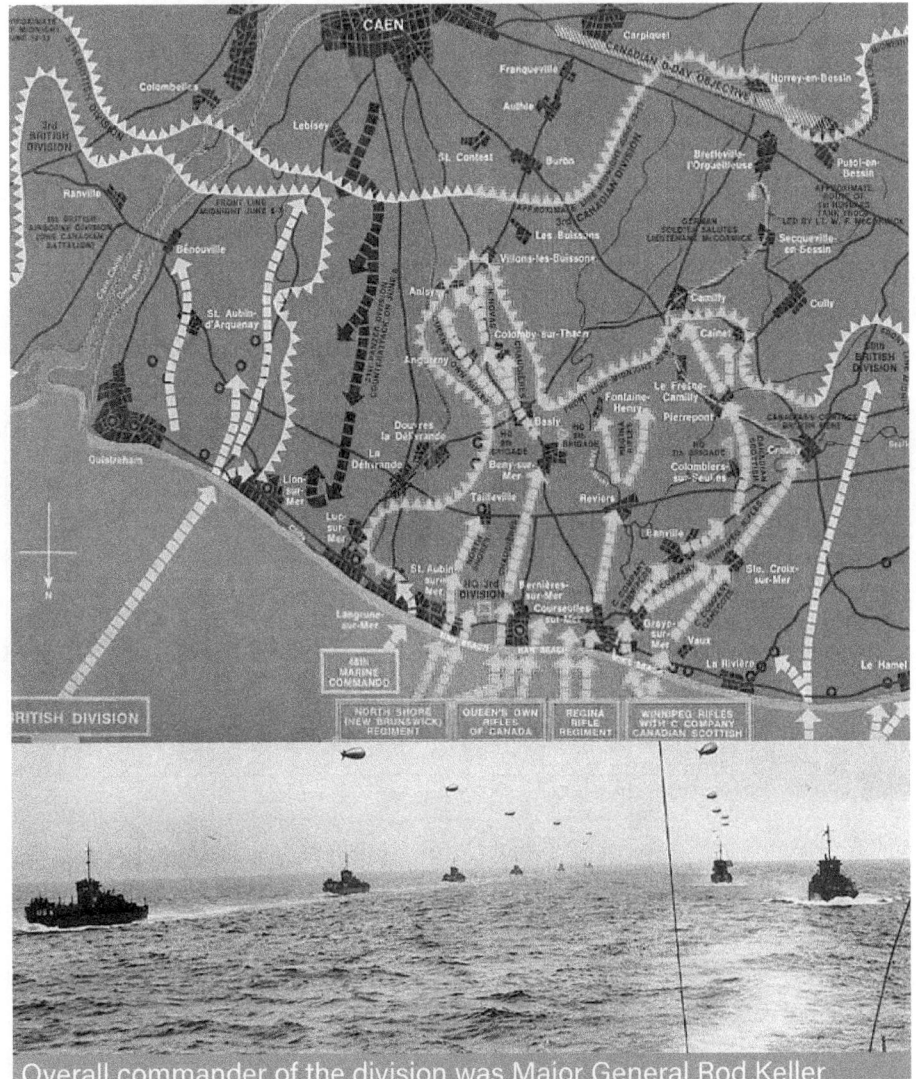

Overall commander of the division was Major General Rod Keller whose immediate superior was General John Crocker. The number of units deployed is on the next page, with casualties, commanders etc.

UNITS	COMMANDER	TOTAL	KIA to July	WOUNDED/ CAPTURED
3rd Infantry Division	Major General Rod Keller	28,845	566 (D-Day) 1,811 (to July)	652 (D-Day) 1,500 (to Jul)
7th Infantry Brigade (1st Wave)	Brigadier Harry Foster	120		Task Force J1
7th Infantry 114 Anti-aircraft Battery Company (Lorne Scots) 372-5 Battery		150	2	
Royal Winnipeg Rifles (Little Black Devils) – Mike Red & Green 07:40-MIKE	Lt Col Meldram (Mike)	880	106	232
A Company (07:45) B Company C Company D Company	Maj F Hodge – St Croix (Red) Capt Gower – Courseulles (Red Maj Jim Jones – St Croix (Green) Maj L Fulton – Reviers (Green)	1st Wave 1st Wave 1st Wave 1st Wave	45 inc. executed by 12SS Panzer	
Regina Rifle Regt –Nan Green – Courseulles NAN 07:45	Lt Col Matheson (Nan Green)	880	186	59
A Company (08:09) B Company (07:58) C Company (08:35) D Company (08:55)	Major Grosch– Courseulles Major Peters – Courseulles Maj S Tubb – Courseulles Major Jack Love – Reviers	1st Wave 1st Wave 2nd Wave 2nd Wave	6 June '44	
1st Battn Canadian Scottish Regt – Pierrepoint – MIKE (07:45)	Lt Col Fred Cabeldu (Mike Red-Green)	880	57	149
A Company (07:45) – Red B Company – Red C Company (08:05) – Green D Company – Green	Maj Plows – Camilly-La Valette Maj Lendrum – LeFresne-Camilly Maj Crofton – Château Vaux Maj MacEwan – St Croix-Reviers	1st Wave 2nd Wave 1st Wave 2nd Wave	23 inc. executed by 12SS Panzer	
8th Infantry Brigade (1st Wave) 07:35	Brigadier Kenneth Blackadder	120		Task Force J2
8th Infantry 73 Anti-Aircraft Co	(Lorne Scots) 219, 220 Batt	150		
Queen's Own Rifles of Canada (Nan White)	Lt Col Spragge	880	168	
A & B Company (1st Wave) C & D Company (2nd Wave)	Major Dalton – Bernières-Anisy Major Nickson & Major Gordon – Bernières, Bény, Colomby, Anguerny Heights			
Régiment de la Chaudière (Nan Red & White)	Lt Col Mathieu	880	85	
A & B Companies – Red	Majors Lapointe & L'Espérance – Bény-sur-Mer			

UNITS	COMMANDER	TOTAL	KIA to July	WOUNDED/ CAPTURED
C & D Companies - White	Majors Sevigny & Taschereau St Aubin and WN27 Lagune- Chateau d'Colomby-sur-Thaon			
North Shore (New Brunswick) Regiment (Nan Red) (07:55)	Lt Col Buell	880	130	158
A & B Companies 1st Wave	Majors Naughton & Forbes – St Aubin and WN27			
C & D Companies 2nd Wave	Majors Daughney & Anderson –Tailleville			
9th Infantry Brigade (Reinforcement)	**Brig. D.G. Cunningham**	**120**		**Task Force J3**
9th Infantry 97 Anti Aircraft Company (Supports 321 Battery)		150	2	
Highland Light Infantry of Canada A, B, C, D - NAN	Lt Col F.M. Griffiths Maj Durnward, Cpt Stark, Maj Hodgins, Maj Anderson – Bridges & Seulles	880	93	
Stormont Dundas & Glengarry Highlanders A, B, C Companies - NAN	Lt Col Christiansen St Croix & Banville; Maj Fisher, Maj Gemmel, Cpt Milligan	880	138	
North Nova Scotia Highlanders A, B, C, D - NAN	Lt Col Charles Petch; Majors Rhodenizer, Wilson, Learment, Matson	880	184	
Cameron Highlanders of Ottawa (Machine Gun Regt) A, B, C, D Companies - MIKE	Lt Col Datchet-Klaehn	880	51	
7th Recon Regt – 17th Duke of York's Royal Canadian Hussars – MIKE	Duke of Edinburgh's Own Lt Col Lewis	135	2	
2nd Armoured Brigade (1st Wave)	**Brigadier R.A. Wyman**	**270**	**1**	
6th Armoured Regiment (1st Hussars) – 40 DD Shermans A, B, C Squadrons - MIKE (133 DD tanks capsized in heavy seas)	Lt Col RJ Colwell (1st Wave)– MIKE Red & Green, NAN Green La Crieux; Major Brookes, Major Duncan & Major Marks	880	85	
10th Armoured Regiment (Fort Garry Horse) 40 DD Shermans A, B, C Squad-NAN	Lt Col REA Morton (1st Wave) –NAN Red & White - Berniers; ?, ?, Major Bray	880	54	12

UNITS	COMMANDER	TOTAL	KIA to July	WOUNDED/ CAPTURED
27th Armoured Regiment (Sherbrooke Fusilier Regt) 40 Firefly Sherman; A, B, C Squad + 62nd Anti Tank – NAN	Lt Col Gordon (3rd Wave) St Aubin Major ?,?,?	880	48 incl 11 executed by 12SS	34
3rd Army Field Artillery – Bretteville	**Brigadier P.A.S. Todd (Uncle Stanley)**	**270**		
12th Field Regiment Artillery (Priest Guns x24) (11th, 16th, 43rd Batteries)	Lt Col. Webb – Banville (with 7th Brigade)	440	10	
13th Field Regiment Artillery (Priest Guns x24) (22nd, 78th, 44th Batteries)	Lt Col Clifford; Major Young – Banville (with 7th Brigade)	440	20	
14th Field Regiment Artillery (Priest Guns x24) (34th, 66th, 81st Batteries)	Lt Col Griffin, 8th Major Alkenbrack – Landed 09:25	440	14	
19th Field Regiment Artillery (Priest Guns x24)	Lt Col Clarke, 8th Major Peene – Landed 09:30	440	5	
3rd Anti Tank Regiment (17 pounder x48) (4th, 52nd, 94th, 106th Batteries)	Lt Col J.P. Phin	440	19	
4th Light Anti Aircraft Regt (40mm Bofors guns x44) (32nd, 69th, 100th Batteries)	Lt Col C. Woodrow.	440	8	
3rd Anti Tank Regt Workshop		440	1	
1st Polish Armoured Reinforcements	**General Stanislav Maczek**	**Black Division**		
10th Polish Dragoons	Lt Col W. Zgorzelski	720		
24th Polish Lancers	Lt Col J. Kanski	720		
10th Polish Mounted Recon Rifles (Cromwell Tanks)	Major J. Maciejowski	440		
N° 48 Royal Marine Commando (landed 08:10) Lt Col Moulton – NAN Red – St Aubin-WN26 Lagrune-sur-Mer then WN25, 23, 22		**535**	**71**	**143**
3rd Battery 2nd Royal Marine Troop (Support) 15 Centaur Tanks (J, K, L, M)		220		
4th Battery 2nd Royal Marine Troop (Support) 15 Centaur Tanks (N, O, P, Q)		220		
C Squadron Inns of Court Regiment (Armoured Recon) (28 light tanks, 44 Bren Gun carriers, 41 motorbikes		440		

JUNO BEACH — CANADIAN 3ʳᴰ ARMY DIVISION

UNITS	COMMANDER	TOTAL	KIA to July	WOUNDED/ CAPTURED
79ᵗʰ Armoured Division (AVRE)	Major General Percy Hobart	130	18	
1- 30ᵗʰ Armoured Brigade				
1ˢᵗ Lothian & Borders Yeomanry 141ˢᵗ Royal Armoured Corp (Queens Own Royal Kents) B Squadron				
2- 1ˢᵗ Assault Brigade – Churchill AVREs Bulldozers				
5ᵗʰ Assault Regt. - 80ᵗʰ Squad.	Major Wiltshire 7th Brigade	220		
42ⁿᵈ Assault Regt - 16ᵗʰ Squad.	Major Murphy	220		
3- 1ˢᵗ Tank Assault Brigade				
1ˢᵗ Royal Tank Regiment Prince Albert's Own Hussars A, B, C Squadrons	Buffaloes			
42ⁿᵈ Royal Tank Regiment London & East Surrey Regts A, B, C Squadrons	Buffaloes			
49ᵗʰ Royal Tank Regiment Royal Northumberland Fusiliers A, B, C Squadrons	RAM Kangaroos			
Royal Canadian Ordnance Corp		880		
Royal Canadian Engineers	Lt Col R.S. Cassidy	270		
5ᵗʰ Field Company RCE		530	10	
6ᵗʰ Field Company RCE		530	17	
16ᵗʰ Field Company RCE		530	6	
18ᵗʰ Field Company RCE		530	6	
3ʳᵈ Canadian Bridge Platoon RCE Pioneer Company		270	1	
3ʳᵈ Road Construction Co.		530		
3ʳᵈ Field Park Company				
27ᵗʰ, 262ⁿᵈ Field Engineer Companies		260		
TAC HQ 80AA Battery RA, A Flight 652 OP Squadron				
156-160 AA Ops Rooms 2x TPS 474 Searchlight Battery				
№ 7 Beach Group (NAN) Supports 7ᵗʰ Infantry Brigade				

UNITS	COMMANDER	TOTAL	KIA to July	WOUNDED/ CAPTURED
619th Sapper Independent Field Company- Bernières.		220		
RAMC Field Ambulance 13, 14, 22, 23		350	11	
RAMC 1, 2 Dressing, 3 Sanitary Unit, 13, 14 Transf., 39, 40, 55 Surg.		350		
RAOC 45 Ammunition Coy, 7, 14 Beach Depots, 139th Issues, Pioneers, 190, 225, 243, 293		350		
RE, 20th Beach Recovery, 72, 85th Engineers, 240th Petrol, 282 Transport, 11th Port, 19th Stores		350		
242nd Provost Company		220		
RAF 107th Beach Section, Royal Navy, Beach Commando L, P, S.		100		
8th Battalion Kings Regiment (Irish)		440	12	
Royal Canadian Signals				
№ 2 DP Wireless Section RCS		135	8	
№ 3 Wireless Section RCS		135	8	
№ 3 Divisional Signals		135	8	
№ 4 Wireless Section RCS		135	6	
№ 8 Beach Group (NAN) Supports 8th Infantry Brigade				
5th Battalion Royal Berkshire Regiment		440	13	
Royal Navy 19 Signals, Commando Unit P. RAF 947 Beach Flight		100		
RAMC - 32, 34 Dressing, 32nd Casualty		150		
RASC - 140 Dental, 30, 199 Transport, 242 Petrol, 4 Ordnance		250		
Pioneers - 15, 144, 170 Companies		150		
RE - 23rd Recovery, 20 Field, 1034 Port, 20th Stores, 59th Equipment, 966 Waterways.		225		
242nd Provost Company		220		

Embarkation Southampton:
7th Brigade C7 HMS Langford (J10), Llangibby Castle (J11), Laird Castle.
8th Brigade C8 HMCS Prince David, J36), SS Minowa (J30), SS Isle of Guernsey (J33), HMS St Hellier (J35), HMS Duke of Wellington (J32).

Embarkation Stokes Bay:
9th Brigade LCTs SS Minowa (J30), HMCS Ulsterman A12 A13 A14 A5 A16 A17 A10. 2nd Armoured Brigade Gosport Hards and Stokes Bay Hards LCTs.
3rd Field Artillery A1 A3 A4 SS Canterbury (J12), SS Ulster Monarch (J18), SS Clan Lamont (J31). No.7 Beach Group SS Llangibby Castle. No.8 Beach Group HMCS Prince David.

CHAPTER 5

CANADIAN 3RD DIVISION
ACTIONS AND OPERATIONS

Following the Allied bombardment the first wave of the 7th and 8th Brigades landed at 07:35 hrs. The Royal Winnipeg Rifles and the Queen's Own Rifles of Canada supported by 1st Hussar DD tanks took heavy casualties in the opening minutes. Heavy artillery support cleared most of the coastal defences within two hours. The reserves of the 7th and 8th Brigades began to deploy at 08:30 hours with the Royal Marines, while the 9th Brigade began its deployment at 11:40 hours with DD tanks of the Sherbrooke Fusiliers. The subsequent push inland towards Carpiquet and Caen-Bayeux railway line achieved mixed results. They were small beaches so traffic backed up on the beach and this delayed the 9th Brigade landings. The 7th Brigade encountered heavy initial opposition heading south to make contact with the 50th Division at Creully. The 8th Brigade encountered heavy resistance at Tailleville.

Further Operations – action at Le Mesnil-Patry 11th June, the Canadians took Carpiquet Aerodrome in July, Operation Totalize 9th August, taking St. Lambert-sur-Dives in August, VC Major Currie, Corridor of Death – Moissey Ford, Hill 140 Action with British Columbian Brigade. Normandy campaign finished with link up with 1st Polish Armoured Brigade closed Falaise Gap on 21st August 1944.

CHAPTER 6

GERMAN FORCES AND UNITS DEFENSIVE POSITIONS
MAIN FORCE – 15TH & 7TH GERMAN ARMIES DEFENSIVE POSITIONS.

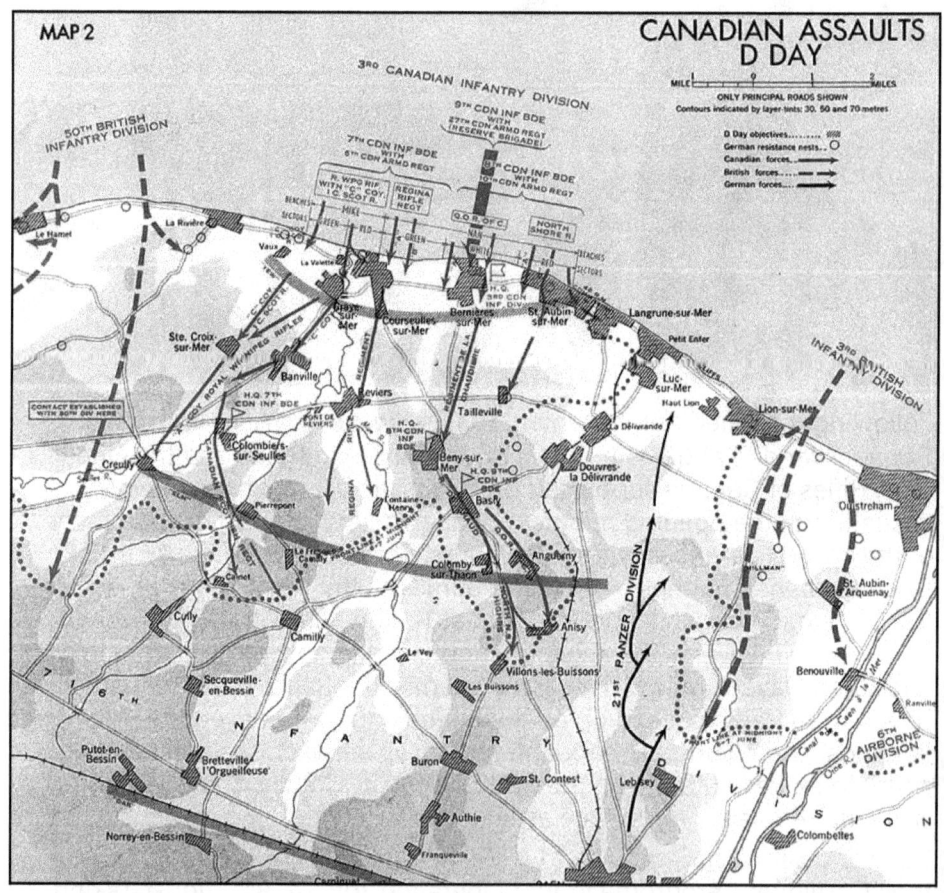

Built by German labour organisation TODT, part of the Atlantic Wall from Norway to Spain, using forced labour gangs. They built strong fortifications called Wilderstandnesten, abbreviated to WN. ("Strong points" – see map). Henri Brunet prepared local drawings for TODT in Caen.

COASTAL DEFENCES

- WN024 – WN025 Luc-sur-Mer – 2 Machine Gun Bunkers 736th 5th and 12th Company 234th Infantry Regiment.
- WN026 – Langrune-sur-Mer – WFMG x3 WF58C Ringsted 50mm anti-tank 736th & 9th (48 Royal Marine Commando).
- WN027 – St Aubin-sur-Mer – 1x 50mm Pak42 Field Guns on Coast, 7 pillboxes & 6x MG42 Machine Gun Nests – n736th 6th Company. Coast St Aubin to Bernières – 12x MG42 (North Shore)
- WN028 Bernières-sur-Mer – 50mm Ringsted and KWK40 8 Pillboxes, 8 machine gun nests 736th 5th Company.
- Coast Bernières to Courseulles-sur-Mer – 10 machine gun nests (Queens Own Rifles).
- WN029 Courseulles-sur-Mer – West Side – 1x 88mm + 2x 75mm FK23 Guns n736th 6th Company + Machine Guns (Regina).
- WN030 Courseulles-sur-Mer – 441th Battalion 2x Ringsted 50mm Field Guns, 2x VF58c, 2x 50mm KWK, 2x 75mm Inland (Regina Rifles).
- WN031 Croix de Lorraine – 1x 75mm MFR 2x 50mm Field Guns, 736th 6th Company 34 machine gun nests along the coast.
- WN032 Vaux (on coast) 50mm KWK 736th 7th Company.
- WN33A Ver-sur-Mer R612 75mm FK.

INLAND DEFENCES

- Reviers – HQ 2nd Battalion 736th Regiment, WN 28A pillboxes – Bunker
- Bazenville – HQ 441st Regiment OST Battalion, plus pillboxes
- Tailleville – 2nd Battalion 736th Regiment HQ, plus machine gun nests, WN23A – Large Bunker, plus 2x 88mm
- La Crieux en Pierre – Pillbox x2, 736th Regiment, 8 companies.
- Creully – 4x Pak42 Field Guns, along river towards Colombiers-sur-Seulles.
- Bény-sur-Mer – 4x Pak 42 Field Guns, north along road to Creully.
- Putot-en-Bessin – 726th Infantry Regiment – road from Creullly – 2x Pak42, 1st Comp-ny 200th Anti Tank Regiment.
- Putot-en-Bessin – 726th Infantry Regiment – north on railway line – 2nd Company 200th Anti Tank Regiment
- Pierrepoint – 3rd Company 200th Anti Tank Regiment – south above crossroads, road between Creully and Carnilly.
- Camilly – 8th Company 192nd Regiment plus 2x Pak42.
- Buron – 6th Company 192nd Regiment.
- Luc-sur-Mer – 12th Company 736th Regiment.
- WN 022 Dourves – Wasserman (Les Moulinex) 2x 100mm Field Guns.
- WN 023A Douvres-la-Délivrande – Freya – large bunkers, protecting Radar Station 2x 100mm Field Guns.
- Anguerny – 92nd Regiment HQ, 9th Company 200th Regiment Anti Tanks.
- Anisy – 5th Company 192nd Panzer Grenadiers.

DEFENSIVE POSITIONS (COASTAL)

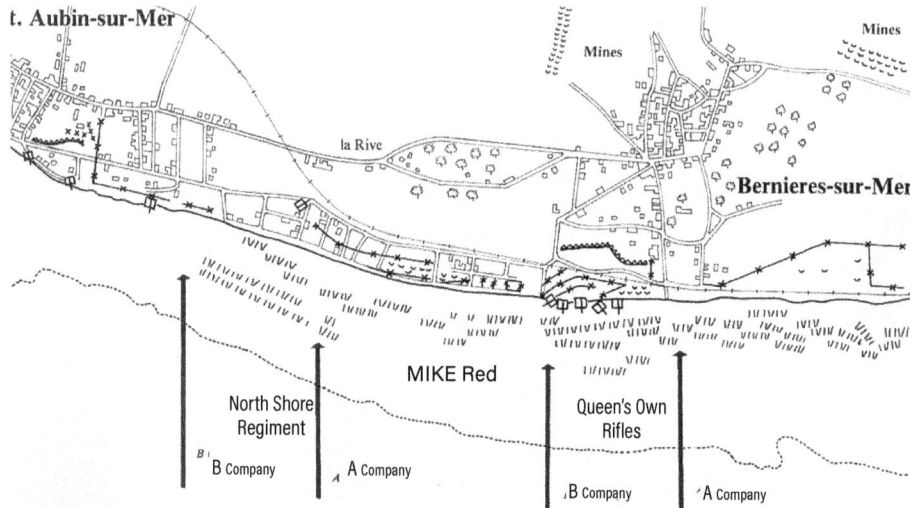

MIKE Red – B Company of the Winnipeg Rifles were engaged 700 yards off shore Graye-sur-Mer; there were heavy casualties whist landing under heavy fire. A Squadron of the 1st Hussars launched their DD Tanks, 1500 yards off shore but were unable to support Winnipeg's for 6 minutes after landing.

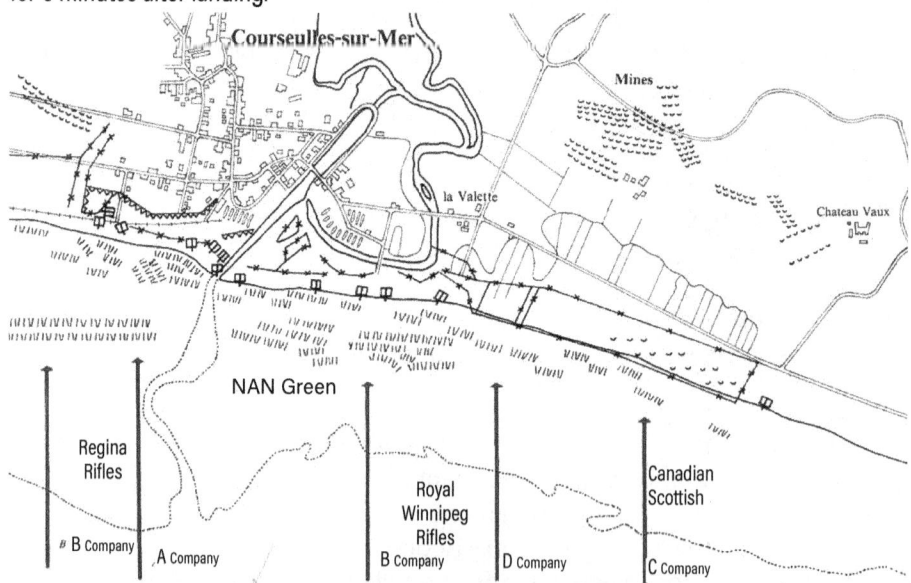

NAN Green – Courseulles – Regina Rifles A Company landed 08:09, waited for 1st Hussars for 20 minutes heavy casualties, B Company landed 07:58, destroyed strong point with B Squadron 1st Hussars. C Company landed 08:35 moved to Courseulles to support A & B. D Company had heavy mortar shelling and mines, only 49 men landed on the beach.

JUNO BEACH — CANADIAN 3ʳᴰ ARMY DIVISION

Left: German Panther Panzers

Right: German Nebelwerfer 42 rocket launcher

DEFENSIVE POSITIONS (INLAND)

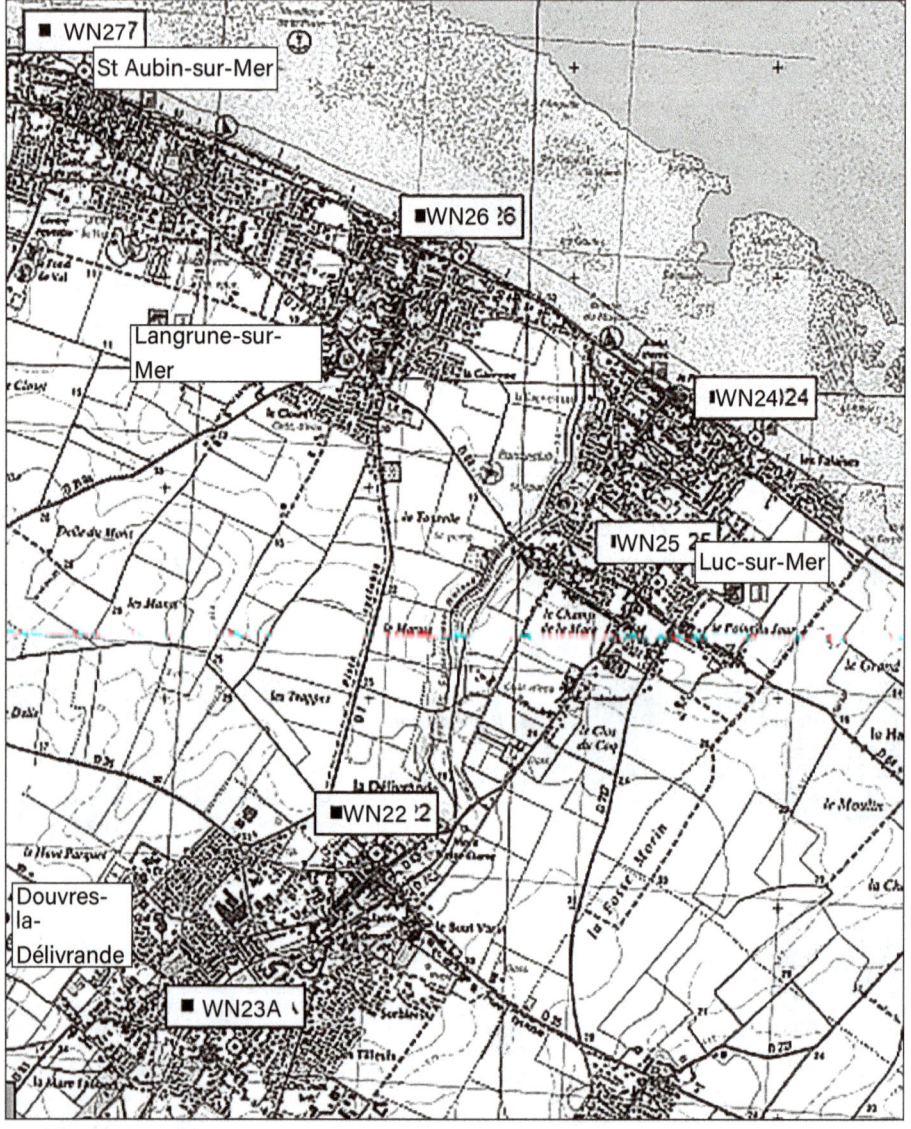

Juno Beach - WN28 Bernières-sur-Mer

Juno Beach - WN27 St Aubin-sur-Mer

Juno Beach - WN33A Graye-sur-Mer

Juno Beach - WN24 Langrune-sur-Mer

Juno Beach - WN31 Courseulles

Juno Beach - WN29 Courseulles-sur-Mer

CHAPTER 7

GERMAN FORCES UNITS COMMANDERS

MAIN FORCE – 7th German Army, above River Dives 15th Army Pas-de-Calais – commanded by Field Marshall Erwin Rommel

1: 716TH INFANTRY DIVISION: LEUT. GENERAL WILHELM RICHTER
- 726th Infantry Regiment – 4th Company – Bernières.
- 736th Infantry Regiment – 5th Company – WN24 & 25 Luc-sur-Mer, WN28 Bernières, 6th Company WN27 St Aubin, WN29 Courseulles, 9th Company WN26 – Langrune, 11th Company – WN23 & WN23A Dourves, 12th Company WN22 Luc-sur-Mer.
- 441st Ost Battalion – WN30 Courseulles.
- 1260th Artillery – 2nd Battery – WN29 &WN30 Courseulles.   TOTAL 1,800 men.

2: 21ST PANZER DIVISION: LEUT. GENERAL FUECHTINGER
- 192nd Panzer Grenadiers – 6th Company – Ainsy, 8th Company – Cairon, HQ – Augerny.
- 220nd Panzer Tank Regiment – HQ Company, 5th Company, 6th Company, 7th Company & 8th Company – Cagny – 10x Mark 4s.
- Sturmgeschütz-Abteilung 200 – Battery 1 & 2 – Putot-en-Besson, 3rd Battery Creully, 4th Battery – Cairon.
- 125th Panzer Grenadiers, 2 Czech Tanks, 4x Mark 4s – Troarn.
- Panzer-Abteilung 21 – 3rd and 9th Flak Battery – Courseulles.   TOTAL 1,750

3: 12SS PANZER DIVISION: HITLER JEUGEN - GENERAL VON SCHWEPPENBURG
- 25th SS Panzer Grenadiers – Lt Oberst Kurt Meyer 2nd Battalion – 2nd, 5th & 6th Companies Troarn. 24x Panthers.
- 26th SS Panzer Grenadiers – Lt Oberst Max Wünsche – 1st, 2nd, & 3rd Companies – Troarn 10x Panzerjägers, 14x Panthers.   TOTAL 2,700

4: REINFORCEMENTS
- 9th SS Panzers – Leut Colonel Otto Meyer – 1st Company 38x StuGs – N12 from Caen, 2nd Company – 30x Panthers.
- 102nd SS Heavy Panzers – Leut Oberst Graffin – 28x Tiger 1 – N12 from Caen.   TOTAL 3,550

TOTAL 9,800 men

CHAPTER 8

FRENCH RESISTANCE OPERATIONS & SPECIAL OPERATIONS EXECUTIVE

SPECIAL OPERATIONS EXECUTIVE (SOE)

This was set up in 1940 under the orders of Winston Churchill to bring the war to the Germans, its objective was to co-ordinate all activity by way of subversion and sabotage against the enemy overseas. The SOE was split by country. Section RF worked with General de Gaulle and the free French in London, Section F (France) was the main section but did not co-ordinate with de Gaulle at the beginning. Agents were sent to France by parachute or Westland Lysander light aircraft. Their job was to train and co-ordinate operations by the French Resistance.

D-Day orders **Operation Hardtack 21** issued on the 11th of January 1944 was to gather intelligence on the following:

- BEACHES – firmness of the beaches, samples of sand, nature of the runes of the beach.
- WALL – nature of sea walls, heights above tide low/high water, obstacles for infantry.
- DUNES – cover for infantry, movement and recognition for each.
- FLOODS – limits of flooded areas, depth, extent and acres.
- ROADS – condition, location of all roads and tracks.
- DEFENCES – obstacles, wire defences, mines, machine gun emplacements, location and complements.

Tackling Beach Obstacles

General Hobart's Funnies

Major General Hobart – 79th Armoured Division.

His task was to come up with a range of equipment that could combat all beach obstacles. From Deddington in Oxfordshire, he came out of retirement and formed a separate division who developed and trained on the weapons below to overcome obstacles.

- Flame Throwers for pillboxes – Churchill Tanks
- Flail Tank for mines – Centaur and Churchill Tanks.
- Sea Walls – Churchill Tank.

Maj Gen Hobart

GENERAL HOBART'S FUNNIES

Flame Throwers for pillboxes – Churchill Tanks

Flail Tank for mines – Centaur and Churchill Tanks.

Sea Walls – Churchill Tank.

CHAPTER 9
RCAF BOMBING OPERATIONS

The Royal Canadian Air Force were based in the United Kingdom assigned to 83 Group Fighter Wing of 3 squadrons of 18 aircraft (39 officers and 743 ranks). Attached to 126, 127, 143 and 144 Canadian Fighter Wings. 143 Squadron flew Typhoon 1B fighter bombers carrying 500 and 1000 lb bombs. Other squadrons flew Spitfire 1XB. 401 Squadron spitfires protected beaches. 438 Squadron Typhoons dive-bombed concrete block houses. Operations 4-6th.

Taxable – 617 Squadron drops window (Chaff) to jam German radar.

Glimmer – 218 Squadron drops window (Chaff) as above.

June 6th – 438 Squadron – Hawker Typhoons, destroyed bunkers.

June 6th – 401 Squadron – Spitfires, protected beaches.

Rob Roy – resupply beach troops and paratroopers.

Aircraft Allocated – 1,136 sorties 5,268 tonnes of bombs.

CHAPTER 10

ROYAL CANADIAN NAVAL OPERATIONS
OPERATION NEPTUNE – D-DAY

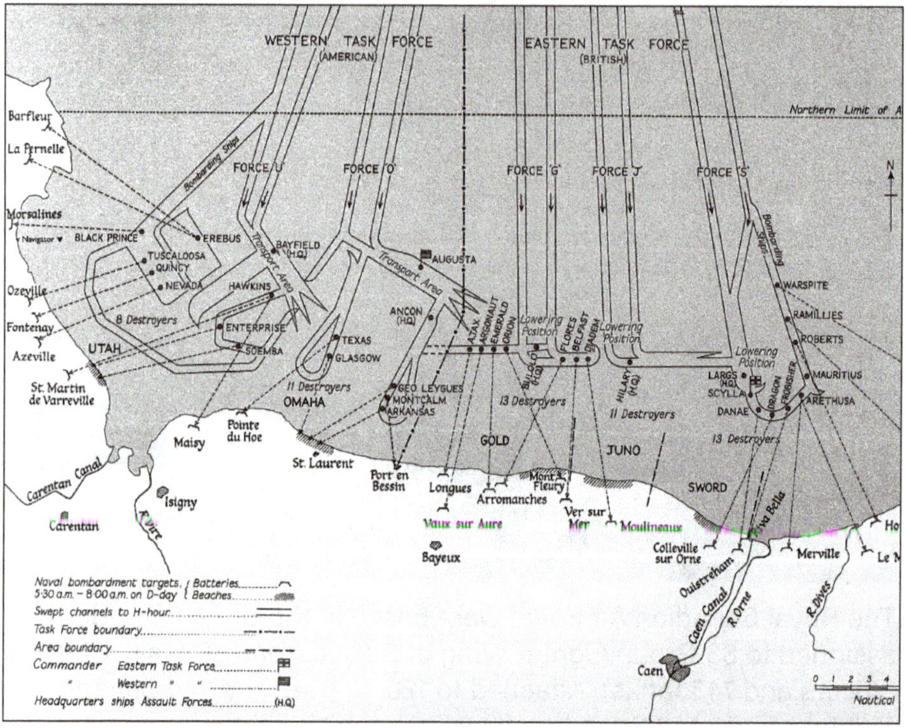

EASTERN TASK FORCE – ASSAULT FORCE "J"

Admiral Sir Bertram Ramsay was appointed Naval Commander-in-Chief of the Allied Naval Expeditionary Force for Operation Neptune.

Rear Admiral Sir Phillip L Vian, commander of the Eastern Task Force (in HMS Scylla), supporting the D-Day landings in Normandy.

Total Ships Eastern Task Force: 1,491 vessels

SHIPS USED AT JUNO BEACH
COMMODORE G.N.OLIVER – HMS HILARY

- BATTLESHIPS CRUISERS (Bombardments) HMS Belfast, Diadem.
- DESTROYERS (V Class) HMCS Algonquin and HMCS Sioux.
- TRIBAL CLASS DESTROYERS HMCS Haida, Huron, Iroquois, Athabaskan (sank 29.4.44), HMS Kempenfet, Faulknor, Venus, Fury, Vigilant, Bleasdale, Glaisdale, Stevenstone, FFS La Combattante (French).
- DESTROYERS HMCS Assinibone, Chaudière, Gatineau, Kootenay, Ottawa, Qu'Appelle, Saskatchewan, Skeena, St Laurent, Restigouche, USS Meville.
- FRIGATES HMCS Cape Breton, Grou, Matane, New Waterford, Outremont, Meon, Port Colborne, Stormont, Saint John, Swansea, Teme, Waskesiu, HMS Lawford, Blairmore.
- MINESWEEPERS HMCS Caraquet, Canso, Bayfield, Cowichan, Fort William, Georgian, Guysborough, Kenora, Malpeque, Milltown, Minas, Mulgrave, Thunder, Vegreville, Wasaga, Queen of Thanet.
- ASDEC TRAWLERS 13 of them.
- CORVETTE HMCS Alberni, Baddeck, Calgary, Camrose, Drumheller, Kitchener, Lindsay, Lunenburg, Mayflower, Mimico, Moosejaw, Rimouski, Port Arthur, Prescott, Regina, Summerside, Trentonian, Woodstock.
- MOTOR TORPEDO BOAT 29th MTB Flotilla – 459, 460, 461, 462, 463, 464, 465, 466.
- MTB FLOTILLA (65 ton) 726, 727, 735, 743, 746, 745, 748.
- LANDING CRAFT
  - Assault Group J1 – HMS Lawford (Llangibby Castle, Prince Henry, Queen Emma, Canterbury, Duke of Argyll, Invicta, Isle of Thanet, Laird's Isle, Mecklenburg, Ulster Monarch + LCH 2 + LCT 48
  - Assault Group J2 – HMS Waveney (SS Lamont, Monowai, Prince David, Biarritz, Brigadier, Duke of Wellington, SS Isle of Guernsey, Lady of Mann, St Helier – 1x LCHQ + 48x LCT).
  - Assault Group J3 – HMS Royal Ulsterman (23x LST, 3x LC Flak 36x LCT 18x LCI. 16x Minesweepers.
  - Royal Marines HMS Prince Albert & SS Princess Margaret.
  - Landing Ships Infantry – HMCS Prince Henry – 528th LCA Flotilla – 856, 1372, 736, 1033, 850, 1021, 925, 1371. HMCS Prince David – 529th LCA Flotilla – 1150, 1375, 1059, 1151, 1138, 1137.
  - Landing Craft Infantry (Large) – 260th Flotilla – LC 1117, 1121, 1166, 1177, 1249, 1266, 1271, 1277, 1285, 1298, 1301. – 262nd Flotilla – 1115, 1118, 1125, 1135, 1250, 1252, 1262, 1263, 1270, 1276, 1299, 1306. 264th Flotilla – LCA 1255, 1288, 1295, 1302, 1305, 1310, 1311.
  - Landing Craft Tanks – 57 in total carried 4 Priest self-propelled guns
  - Landing Craft (10), Flak(11), Smokers (6), Vehicles (67), Obstacles (4), Hedgerows (18). Troop Ships – SS Monoway, Isle of Thanet, Laird Isle, Canterbury, Llangybby Castle, HMS Calshot, HMS Frobisher.

TOTAL Vessels JUNO: 439

CHAPTER 11

D-DAY ACTIONS
WRITE UP ON LANDINGS.
TIMELINE: JUNO BEACH 6TH JUNE 1944

» 05:35 German shore batteries open fire; Allied naval forces, now massed along entire Normandy coast, begin bombardment.

» 06:30 Assault on beaches starts. 3rd Canadian Division landing on Juno made more difficult by strong current. Delay allows Germans to mount strong defence. Objective : advance inland and join troops from British beaches.

» 07:00 German radio broadcasts first report of landing.

» 07:45 1st Battalion Canadian Scots land at Mike Red.

» 07:45 1st Battalion Royal Winnipeg Rifles land at Mike Red .

» 08:05 Regina Rifles land Nan Green and attack WN29.

» 08:05 Queen's Own Riffles of Canada land and struggle at Bernières.

» 08:10 North Shore (New Brunswick) land at St Aubin.

» 08:30 48 Commando lands at St Aubin, Juno Beach and heads east. Beach clearance difficult due to high tides and rough seas.

» 09:00 General Eisenhower issues communiqué announcing start of invasion.

» 09:35 Canadian 8th Brigade liberates Bernières.

» 11:12 After fierce fire fight, 7th Brigade secures Juno exit at Courseulles. But congestion as Canadian 9th Brigade arrives.

» 11:20 Canadians capture Tailleville, Banville and St Croix.

» 12:00 As Winston Churchill reports landings to House of Commons, further landings on Juno. Langrune captured by Juno troops.

» 13:35 German 352nd Division wrongly advises HQ that Allied assault repulsed. Message not corrected until 18.00.

» 14:15 All Canadian 3rd Division now ashore on Juno. Rapid advances start: troops link with those from Gold.

» 18:00 3rd Canadian Division, North Nova Scotia Highlanders reach three miles inland. 1st Hussar tanks cross Caen-Bayeux railway, 10 miles inland. Canadian Scottish link with 50th Division at Creully.

» 20:00 Canadians from Juno Beach reach Villons-les-Buissons, seven miles inland. Attack by 21st Panzers reach coast between Sword and Juno at Luc-sur-Mer.

» 22:00 Rommel returns to HQ from Germany. Montgomery sails for France.

Aim of capturing Carpiquet airfield not achieved. No link yet with Sword forces.

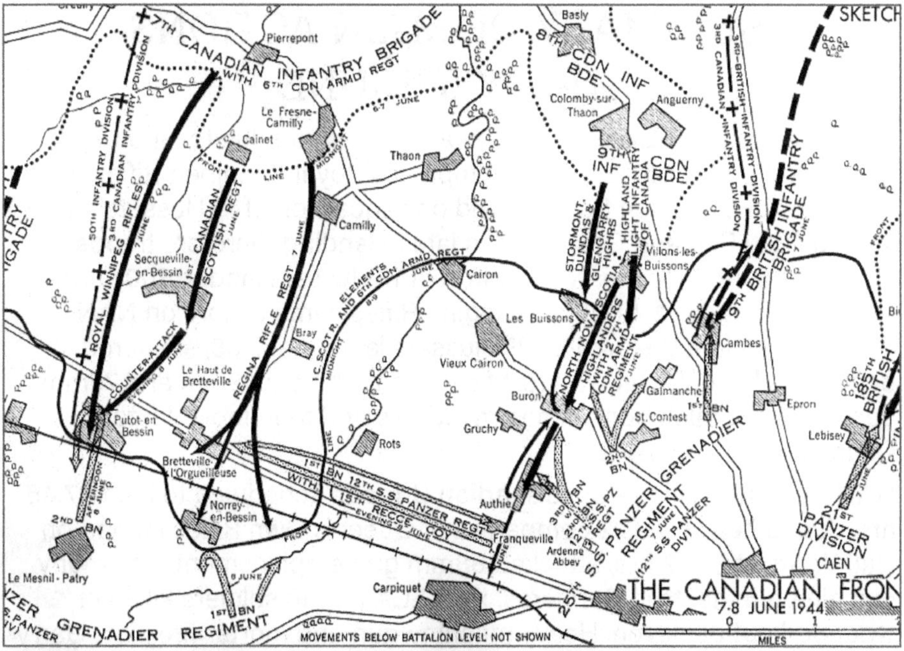

JUNO BEACH — CANADIAN 3RD ARMY DIVISION

Château d'Audrieu today

Kurt Meyer on trial for War Crimes, sentenced to death, but commuted on appeal. (Also Authie executions)

EXECUTIONS – Le Château d'Audrieu at Brouay.

On the 7th of June the Winnipeg Rifles and Regina Rifles had taken up a position at Putot-en-Bessin at 13:30 hrs. The flank had opened up as the 9th Brigade failed to take Carpiquet airport. The 12SS Panzer Grenadiers (Hitler Juegen) under Colonel Kurt Meyer mounted a counter attack which was repelled, but the second counter attack that night 8th of June encircled Putot-en-Bessin with tanks, and captured C Company. The soldiers were marched off to the Château d'Audrieu at Brouay and during the night taken out in groups and shot – 45 Winnepegs, and 23 Canadian Scottish.

SUMMARY OF MAIN ACTIONS
D-DAY 6TH JUNE

MIKE Red to NAN Green – 7TH Canadian Brigade due to land 07:35 hrs; engagement assaults by 2 companies Royal Winnipeg Rifles and Company of Canadian Scottish and one squadron of 1st Hussars' tanks landed Mike Red and Green; tanks late in landing therefore troops landed under heavy fire. A Squadron of 1st Hussars landed 700 yards out, got to beach at 08:15 hrs. Regina Rifles came ashore on NAN Green, tanks late B squadron 1st Hussars landed at 7:58, sheltered behind wall, then dealt with fortifications that held 88mm and 75mm guns in 4 foot thick bunker, destroyed this and then moved into Courselles.

NAN Red and White – 8TH Canadian Brigade scheduled to land 07:45 hrs, due to heavy seas 2 companies of Queen's Own Rifles landed on Nan White at 08:12 hrs, attacked 88mm gun emplacement with many machine gun nests in Bernières. First LCA had 10 soldiers killed or wounded out of eleven. Heavy machine gun and mortar fire. Fort Garry Horse DD tanks arrived and gave fire support and outflanked guns and machine gun nests – 65 casualties. The North Shore Regiment's two companies landed at 08:10 hrs at St Aubin, the strong point had not been touched by Naval gun fire and the soldiers had a 100 yard dash in face of heavy fire. The concrete casements were thick. At 08:20 the Fort Garry DD tanks and AVRE tanks landed at Nan Red, destroyed mines and eliminated the strong point.

The reserves landed at 08:30 hrs Le Régiment de la Chaudière and North Shore and QOR, together with 48 Royal Marine Commando. 48 Royal Marine Commando bypassed action in Saint Aubin and headed to Langrune-sur-Mer which they attacked. The fortification had not been touched and they incurred 40% casualties before taking the strong point with some tank support.

WN 27 St Aubin-sur-Mer

WN 28 Bernières-sur-Mer

CHAPTER 12

D-DAY ACTIONS
7ᵀᴴ INFANTRY BRIGADE & 6ᵀᴴ ARMOURED
(1ˢᵀ HUSSARS 40 DD TANKS)

1. 7ᵀᴴ CANADIAN RECON REGIMENT

(17th Duke of York Canadian Hussars) Beach exit reconnaissance parties divided into two. TC (Traffic Control) painted on their helmets. Their job was look for vehicle exits off the beach. Launched from ship at 06:30 hrs. They directed bulldozers, flails and built exits for troops. Equipment of Landing Craft Assaults. Each contact detachment consisted of an Officer, Corporal, two wireless operators, a Jeep and 2 wireless sets and batteries, assigned to each company commander. By 15:00 hours all major work was finished.

2. ROYAL WINNIPEG (Little Black Devils) Disembarked from the Laird Isle, Canterbury and Llangybby Castle onto Mike Red & Green at 07:45 hrs at the edge of Courseulles. Heavy fire on tanks. Bombardment failed to knock out any German position. WN31 – Tasks: 5 major casements and 15 pillboxes. Hard defence B Company with 6th Field Engineers cleared mines (lost all men bar 26). Pillbox on west side of the river Seulles with 75mm gun was rushed by Corporal Klos, killed 2 before dying and was destroyed. D Company moved quickly off the beach cleared path through minefield to La Vallette under Major Fulton then Graye-sur-Mer. A company moved to Croix-sur-Mer. C Company to Banville cleared 3 machine guns with the help from 6th Armoured, then with 1st Hussars Saint Croix-sur-Mer, Banville, Creully, then met up at Pierrepoint link up with units from Gold.

3. REGINA RIFLES Embarked on Isle of Thanet, landed at Nan Green at Courseulles. Task: Take WN29 and WN31. (Hard) A Company at 08:05 hrs. B Company at 08:15 hrs, in front of the sea wall. Coursuelles had been divided into 12 blocks. A company ordered to take gun emplacement Block 1 off beach mouth of River Seulles, then along the canal 5, 6, and 7, either side of the river. Block 2 gun emplacement followed by 4, 8, 9, 10, 11, 12 Companies. 14 out of 20 tanks landed at 08:30 hrs and helped take WN29 and WN31B. Then move on Reviers at 11:00 hrs to take WN30, taken at 15:00 hrs with Companies C and D with tanks. At 18:00 hrs took Fontaine-Henry with B and C Company.

4. 1ST BATTALION CANADIAN SCOTS – Mike Red Beach, at Courseulles. C Company under command Royal Winnipeg's landed at 07:49 hrs at the junction of Mike & Love under heavy fire. Bypassed WN31 assaulted the fortified Châteaux at Vaux. Large gun emplacement knocked out by the Royal Navy. Lieutenant Schjelderup attacked three German machine gun nests and took 15 prisoners. One prisoner led the Canadian Scots through a minefield to fields beyond.

8TH INFANTRY & 10TH ARMOURED BRIGADES
FORT GARRY TANKS (40 DD TANKS)

1. **QUEEN'S OWN RIFLES** – on the SS Monowai, Nan White near Bernières at 08:05 hrs. Task was to take WN28 and the sea wall. Fort Garry DD tanks landed 20 mins later due to rough seas. Some LCAs

hit mines. The AVREs landed with troops cleared mines. A Company hit by heavy machine guns and mortar fire, but got off beach quickly and began clearing Bernières. B Company had to take the five pillboxes on the sea wall, landed after drifting 200 metres off course. Lieutenant Herbert with Lance Corporal Tessier, Rifleman Chicoski charged the fortification WN28 and destroyed the bunker with hand grenades and sten guns. DD tanks landed and helped clear pillboxes. AVREs cleared beach exit and moved off 09:30 hrs into town. C & D companies LCA hit mines and landed at 08.45 hrs with casualties. Moved on to take Ainsy, Beny, Colomby, Anguerny. Three Westlake brothers from this regiment buried in Beny cemetery, HQ in La Maison, Bernières.

2. **LE RÉGIMENT DE LA CHAUDIÈRE** – landed at Nan White near Bernières at 08:30 hrs, their task was to pass through QOR and head south, attack Germans on the way. 4 out of the 5 landing craft damaged by concealed mines. By 10:30 hrs formed up with A Squadron Fort Garry Tanks and 14th Field Artillery three M7 Priest guns. Moved towards

Beny-sur-Mer, surrounded by mine fields. Attacked by 88mm guns, destroyed all Priest guns. Lt Moisan from A Company attacked and destroyed 88mm gun in Beny. with B & C company took Beny by mid afternoon. D Company reached Basly. C Company La Mare capturing 4 vehicles and 20 prisoners. B Company attacked Château de Talleville, HQ 736th German Infantry Regiment HQ. Then moved to Colomby-sur-Thaon and then captured the bridge and 30 Germans and a Colonel. Moved on to WN22 Les Moulineux and WN23 Radar at Douvres-la-Délivrande fortifications with C Squadron Fort Garry Tanks. Later took Carpiquet Airfield in August 1944 (Major Gauvin).

3. **NORTH SHORE REGIMENT** (New Brunswick) – Nan Red St Aubin at 08:10 hrs. from SS Monowai. Attacked WN27, weak defence. Accompanied by C Squadron Fort Garry Tanks, 14th & 19th Field Regiments Artillery with 105mm guns. B company landed at St Aubin take 50mm gun emplacement. Used Bangalore torpedoes, pinned down by heavy mortars, and snipers, heavy casualties. With tanks and AVREs then took fortification. C and D Companies arrived took St Aubin from German 736th regiment. Moved on to Tailleville. Secured defensive position by 22:00 hrs. Then moved on to radar station at Douvres.

9TH INFANTRY BRIGADE. & 27TH ARMOURED SHERBROOKE FUSILIERS

1. **HIGHLAND LIGHT INFANTRY** – support the attack on Carpiquet Airport, (objective line Oak). Attack at Hell's Corner on D220 near Villons-les-Buissons. Cleared Villons and captured a German 88mm gun and a six barrelled mortar 7-8th of June. Hells Corner memorial in Villons-les-Buissons.

Hell's Corner plaque

2. **STORMONT, DUNDAS & GLENGARRY HIGHLANDERS** – Landed on Nan White (actions as above).

3. **NORTH NOVA SCOTIA HIGHLANDERS** landed at 11:40 hrs, beach busy, ordered to move to Beny-sur-Mer, severe congestion did not get there until 16:05 hrs. With tanks from Sherbrooke Fusiliers moved south to Villons-sur-Buissons at 20:00 hrs engaged the Germans. Attacked by 12th SS Panzers could not reach Carpiquet Airport. Captured at Authie and 27 executed at Abbaye d'Ardenne by Fritz Witt (12th SS Panzer) with Sherbrooke Fusilers.

4. **CAMERON HIGHLANDERS OF OTTAWA** (Duke of Edinburgh's Own). Four Companies, three machine guns A, B, and C and 1 heavy mortar company, Company D, under Major Ross. Assigned to 9th Brigade. But B Company under Major Carson was assigned to taking St Aubin and then Beny.

2ND ARMOURED BRIGADE

1. 6TH ARMOURED BRIGADE (1st Hussars) accompanied 7th Brigade, offered support to units to captures German fortifications.

2. 10TH ARMOURED BRIGADE (Fort Garry Horse) accompanied 8th Brigade.

3. 27TH ARMOURED BRIGADE (Sherbrooke Fusiliers), accompanied 9th Brigade, objective Carpiquet airfield, beaten back on the 7th of June by 12th SS Panzers, 11 tanks were captured and 18 men executed by the Germans at Abbaye d'Ardenne near Caen.

48 ROYAL MARINE COMMANDO

Landed at 08:30 hrs Nan Red bypassed WN27 at St Aubin and attacked WN26 at Langrune-sur Mer, then made their way inland after meeting up with 41 Royal Marines. Attacked WN23 the Radar installation at Douvres with 22nd Dragoons Tank Company and 26th and 77th Royal Engineers; 3 killed after taking the Radar Station, with 12 Germans killed and 30 wounded.

Attack on WN22 & WN23 Douvres. Bunkers and Radar Station held by Battalion III Oberleut. Heinrich Korzilius. Defences 7x 20mm & 30mm Flak Guns and 6x 50mm and 75mm Anti Tank Guns. Canadians siege fortification until the 41 & 48 Royal Marine Commandos came up with the support of the 22nd Dragoons, Flail Tanks etc. Captured the fortifications on the 9th of July 1944.

OTHER UNITS

SUPPORT DD TANKS – 3rd Canadian Armour, most of the tanks got into the beaches which minimised the casualties and helped destroy German Bunkers.

AVRE CHURCHILL TANKS – clearing obstacles. RE (each squadron had 2 Flails, 3 AVREs and 1 Bulldozer).

THE 6TH FIELD ARTILLERY – cleared the minefields for D Company Winnipeg Rifles as the Flail tanks failed to arrive on time. The Canadian Scottish C Company landed with very little opposition as 75mm guns had been destroyed by naval gun fire on Mike Green and then moved inland to the villages of Banville & St Croix-sur-Mer. They joined up with A Company and destroyed heavy machine guns with the 1st Hussars.

NURSES FROM RCAMC – (Royal Canadian Army Medical Corp) Field Hospitals were set up at Reviers and there were several Field Dressings stations to tend for casualties nearer the battles.

CHAPTER 13

LIST OF CITATIONS

- **Captain Phil Gower:** Military Cross, Royal Canadian Engineers 6th Field Company (6th June 1944) – Bridge over River Seulles with B Company Winnipegs.
- **Corporal "Bull" Klos:** Military Cross (6th June 1944) – B Company Winnipegs – mortally wounded took out German MG42 on River Seulles.
- **Lieutenant Bill Grayson:** Military Cross (6th June 1944) – A Company Regina Rifles – Nan Green – Block 1 River Seulles bunker captured 35 Germans with a charge on the bunker.
- **Lieutenant Herbert:** Military Cross; (6th June 1944) – B Company Queen's Own Rifles – destroyed the main pillbox, with sten guns and grenades firing through the slits on Nan White Beach, Bernières, as company landed directly in front of pillbox.
- **Lance Corporal R. Tessier:** Military Medal (6th June 1944) – (as above)
- **Rifleman W. Chicoski:** Military Medal (6th June 1944) – (as above)
- **Lieutenant Moisan:** Military Cross (6th June 1944) – A Company Regimént de la Chaudière – action taking 88mm gun in hole at Beny-sur-Mer.
- **Major C.O. Dalton:** DSO (7th June 1944) – A Company Queen's Own Rifles of Canada.
- **Sergeant C.W.Smith:** Medal of Merit (7th June 1944) – Queen's Own Rifles.
- **Major David Currie:** Victoria Cross (19th August 1944) – 2nd Canadian Corp, 4th Canadian Armoured Division, South Alberta Regiment – Saint Lambert-sur-Dives, fought off counter attack of German Tanks.

Major Currie earned the Victoria Cross for his efforts on 18 August 1944 to capture and hold the village of St Lambert-sur-Dives during the fighting to block the escape route of large German forces cut off in the Falaise pocket.

Rifleman W. Chicoski after receiving the Military Medal for valour on D-Day

CHAPTER 14

CURRENT MUSEUMS & PLAQUES

- Centre Juno Beach Museum, Courseulles – 0033-2-31.37.32.17 www.junobeach.org. €7.00.
- Musee de Radar, Douvres-la-Delivrande – 0033-2-31.37.74.43 www.musee-radar.fr €5.50.
- Musee Gold Beach - 0033-2-31.22.58.50 www.goldbeachmusee.fr €4.50.
- Canadian Cemetery at Reviers, Bény-sur-Mer – 2,029 graves.
- British Cemetery at Secqueville-en-Bessin – 98 graves.
- British Cemetery at Cambes-en-Plaine – 223 graves.
- British Cemetery at Brouay – 370 graves.
- British Cemetery at Douvres-la-Délivrande – 879 graves.
- Cemetery at Bénouville Church – 23 graves.
- Canadian Cemetery at Bretteville-sue-Laize.
- German Cemetery at La Cambe.
- Tiger 1 Tank at Vimoutiers – actual tank memorial. Abandoned August 1944. (See Wikipedia entry for future restoration plans)

Cross of Lorraine - Courseulles

Cemetry at Secqueville-en-Bessin

JAMES ROBERTSHAW
AUTHOR

Accountant, lives in Witney, with his wife and daughter, has always been interested in Military History, in particular World War II. James is a member of the Royal British Legion. James' aunts and uncles served in the forces during the Second World War. Two of his aunts were in Bletchley Park during the war and his grandfather owned the gardener's house in the park and supplied Bletchley Park with meat and vegetables from his farm. James' mother was a hospital sister during the blitz and nursed troops coming back from the D-Day beaches. His father, Michael served in the RAF but was posted to Burma, he served as an aircraft mechanical instructor in Lord Louis Mount Batten's Squadron.

OTHER BOOKS IN THE SERIES

- 6th British Airborne Landing Operations.
- Sword Beach Operations – 3rd British Division.
- Juno Beach Operations – 3rd Canadian Division.
- Gold Beach Operations – 50th British Division.
- Omaha Beach Operations – 1st and 29th US Divisions and 2nd Ranger Battalion.
- Utah Beach Operations – 4th and 90th US Division.
- US 101st Airborne – Western Flank – Sainte Marie du Mont – Carentan.
- US 82nd Airborne – Western Flank – Sainte-Mère-Église.
- French Resistance and Special Operations Executive (SOE) 1940-44

www.dday-wardiaries.co.uk

Acknowledgements:
Use of old photographs by
permission of Wikipedia

Jan 2023

www.ingramcontent.com/pod-product-compliance
Lightning Source LLC
Chambersburg PA
CBHW070656050426
42451CB00008B/380